ADVA

T0168086

"In this book Greta Christina tackles the subject of death with the insight of a philosopher and the relaxed candor of a friend—that really cool, intelligent friend who understands and cares."

—David Niose, author of *Fighting Back the Right: Reclaiming America from the Attack on Reason*

"This is a book about the philosophy of death that actually confronts the practical reality of it, and helps you come to practical terms with it. . . . The best book on the atheist philosophy of death you are likely ever to read."

—Richard Carrier, author of *On the Historicity of Jesus*

"When I was very young, I lost someone close to me in a car accident. Almost more painful than the loss was the way by which those around me attempted to find meaning in the senseless death of a young person. This is the book that seven-year-old me needed instead of the endless religious tracts that assured me that everything happens for a reason."

—Heina Dadabhoy, Heinous Dealings

"Bravo, Greta Christina. Your book is a feat of logic, wisdom, compassion, insight, humor, and lived experience presented in the most accessible way. Your ideas are compelling and I wish your words could be made available in hotel rooms everywhere, tucked into the drawer of the nightstand, in addition to hospital waiting rooms, train and bus stations, airports and classrooms. Death is certainly a Big Deal but humanism and non-belief have plenty of comfort to offer, as you so eloquently have put forth. In short, 'What she said.'"

—Nina Hartley, author of *Nina Hartley's Guide to Total Sex*

"Greta Christina's new book transcends merely 'enjoyable.' Joy, tranquility, truth—I feel these while reading it."

—Brianne Bilyeu, Biodork

"Atheism frees us to craft our own meaning for life, but we must still confront the specter of death. In this brief-yet-essential volume, Greta Christina presents an array of humanist perspectives that provide very real comfort and meaning in the face of death."

—Neil Wehneman, Development Director, Secular Student Alliance

"Greta Christina continues to provide unique advice and information to the growing community of seculars. We all need to consider our mortality and learn positive and productive ways to deal with our inevitable deadline. Thanks for this little book of wisdom. Christina has written a handbook we can all use. But it should be in the hands of every hospital and military chaplain, every hospice care giver, even ministers, etc. No secular person should be subjected to supernatural ideas and wishful thinking when they are dealing with death, dying and grief."

—Darrel Ray, Founder, Recovering from Religion

"Reading this book felt like one of those moments, standing in a dark and silent room, when glass powder strikes red phosphorous and turns a little of it into white phosphorous, which causes a match to light up in a warming flame. I want to show it (the book, not the match) to all my friends who are dealing with death, which is of course all of my friends. Thank you for writing it!"

—Greg M. Epstein, Humanist Chaplain at Harvard University

COMFORTING THOUGHTS ABOUT DEATH THAT HAVE NOTHING TO DO WITH GOD

COMFORTING THOUGHTS ABOUT DEATH THAT HAVE NOTHING TO DO WITH GOD

GRETA CHRISTINA

PITCHSTONE PUBLISHING
Durham, North Carolina

Pitchstone Publishing
Durham, North Carolina 27705

"Comforting Thoughts About Death That Have Nothing To Do With God"
    originally published in *Skeptical Inquirer*.
"The Meaning of Death, Part One of Many," "The Meaning of Death,
    Part Two of Many: Motivation and Mid-Life Crises," "The Meaning of
    Death, Part Three of Many: Fear, Grief, and Actually Experiencing Your
    Emotions," "Atheism, Death, and the Difference Between Pessimism and
    Realism," and "Atheism and the Argument from Comfort" originally
    published on Greta Christina's Blog.
"Lydia's Cancer, and Atheist Philosophies of Death," "Grief Beyond Belief:
    How Atheists Are Dealing With Death," and "Atheists in Foxholes"
    originally published on *AlterNet*.
"Do We Concede the Ground of Death Too Easily?" originally published in
    Free Inquiry.
"Humanism in a Shitstorm" originally published in *The Humanist*.

To contact the publisher,
please email info@pitchstonepublishing.com

10 9 8 7 6 5 4 3 2 1

Library of Congress Cataloging-in-Publication Data

Christina, Greta.
  Comforting thoughts about death that have nothing to do with God / Greta
Christina.
     pages cm
  ISBN 978-1-939578-18-1 (alk. paper)
  1. Death. 2. Atheism. I. Title.
  BD444.C468 2015
  128'.5—dc23
                                2015015107

Cover design by Alex Gabriel

For Ingrid.

CONTENTS

1

COMFORTING THOUGHTS ABOUT DEATH THAT HAVE NOTHING TO DO WITH GOD

So here's the problem. If you don't believe in God or an afterlife; or if you believe that the existence of God or an afterlife are fundamentally unanswerable questions; or if you do believe in God or an afterlife but you accept that your belief is just that, a belief, something you believe rather than something you know—if any of that is true for you, then death can be an appalling thing to think about. Not just frightening, not just painful. It can be paralyzing. The fact that your lifespan is an infinitesimally tiny fragment in the life of the universe, and that there is, at the very least, a strong possibility that when you die, you disappear completely and forever, and that in five hundred years nobody will remember you and in five billion years the Earth will be boiled into the sun: this can be a profound and defining truth about your existence that you reflexively repulse, that you flinch away from and refuse to accept or even think about, consistently pushing to the back of your mind whenever it sneaks up, for fear that if you allow it to sit in your mind even for a minute, it will swallow everything else. It can make everything you do, and everything anyone else does, seem meaningless, trivial to the point of absurdity. It can make you feel erased, wipe out joy, make your life seem like ashes in your hands. Those of us who are atheists and skeptics and doubters are sometimes dismissive of people who fervently hold beliefs they have no evidence for simply because they find them comforting—but when you're in the grip of this sort of existential despair, it can be hard to feel like you have anything but that handful of ashes to offer them.

But here's the thing. I think it's possible to be an atheist, or an agnostic, or to have religious or spiritual beliefs that you don't have certainty about, and still feel okay about death. I think there are ways to look at death, ways to experience the death of other people and to contemplate our own, that allow us to feel the value of life without denying the finality of death. I can't make myself believe in things I don't actually believe—Heaven, or reincarnation, or a greater divine plan for our lives —simply because believing those things would make death easier to accept. And I don't think I have to, or that anyone has to. I think there are ways to think about death that are comforting, that give peace and solace, that allow our lives to have meaning and even give us more of that meaning—and that have nothing whatsoever to do with any kind of God, or any kind of afterlife.

Here's the first thing. The first thing is time, and the fact that we live in it. Our existence and experience are dependent on the passing of time, and on change. No, not dependent—dependent is too weak a word. Time and change are integral to who we are, the foundation of our consciousness, and its warp and weft as well. I can't imagine what it would mean to be conscious without passing through time and being aware of it. There may be some form of existence outside of time, some plane of being in which change and the passage of time are an illusion, but it certainly isn't ours.

And inherent in change is loss. The passing of time

has loss and death woven into it: each new moment kills the moment before it, and its own death is implied in the moment that comes after. There is no way to exist in the world of change without accepting loss, if only the loss of a moment in time: the way the sky looks right now, the motion of the air, the number of birds in the tree outside your window, the temperature, the placement of your body, the position of the people in the street. It's inherent in the nature of having moments: you never get to have this exact one again.

And a good thing, too. Because all the things that give life joy and meaning—music, conversation, eating, dancing, playing with children, reading, thinking, making love, all of it—are based on time passing, and on change, and on the loss of an infinitude of moments passing through us and then behind us. Without loss and death, we don't get to have existence. We don't get to have Shakespeare, or sex, or five-spice chicken, without allowing their existence and our experience of them to come into being and then pass on. We don't get to listen to Louis Armstrong without letting the E-flat disappear and turn into a G. We don't get to watch *Groundhog Day* without letting each frame of it pass in front of us for a 24th of a second and then move on. We don't get to walk in the forest without passing by each tree and letting it fall behind us; we don't even get to stand still in the forest and gaze at one tree for hours without seeing the wind blow off a leaf, a bird break off a twig for its nest, the clouds moving behind it, each manifestation of the tree dying and a new one taking its place.

And we wouldn't want to have it if we could. The alternative would be time frozen, a single frame of the film, with nothing to precede it and nothing to come after. I don't think any of us would want that. And if we don't want that, if instead we want the world of change, the world of music and talking and sex and whatnot, then it is worth our while to accept, and even love, the loss and the death that make it possible.

Here's the second thing. Imagine, for a moment, stepping away from time, the way you'd step back from a physical place, to get a better perspective on it. Imagine being outside of time, looking at all of it as a whole—history, the present, the future—the way the astronauts stepped back from the Earth and saw it whole.

Keep that image in your mind. Like a timeline in a history class, but going infinitely forward and infinitely back. And now think of a life, a segment of that timeline, one that starts in, say, 1961, and ends in, say, 2037. Does that life go away when 2037 turns into 2038? Do the years 1961 through 2037 disappear from time simply because we move on from them and into a new time, any more than Chicago disappears when we leave it behind and go to California?

It does not. The time that you live in will always exist, even after you've passed out of it, just like Paris exists before you visit it, and continues to exist after you leave. And the fact that people in the 23rd century will probably never know you were alive . . . that doesn't make your life disappear, any more than Paris disappears if your cousin Ethel never sees it. Your segment on that timeline will always have been there. The fact of your death doesn't make the time that you were alive disappear.

And it doesn't make it meaningless. Yes, stepping back and contemplating all of time and space can be daunting, can make you feel tiny and trivial. And that perception isn't entirely inaccurate. It's true: the small slice of time that we have is no more important than the infinitude of time that came before we were born, or the infinitude that will follow after we die.

But it's no less important, either.

I don't know what happens when we die. It seems most likely that we simply disappear, but I don't know for sure. And I don't know that it matters. What matters is that we get to be alive. We get to be conscious. We get to be connected with each other, and with the world, and we get to be aware of that connection and to spend a few years mucking about in its possibilities. We get to have a slice of time and space that's ours. As it happened, we got the slice that has Beatles records and Thai restaurants and AIDS and the Internet. People who came before us got the slice that had horse-drawn carriages and whist and dysentery, or the one that had stone huts and Viking invasions and pigs in the yard. And the people who come after us will get the slice that has, I don't know, flying cars and soybean pies and identity chips in their brains. But our slice is no less important because it comes when it does, and it's no less important because we'll leave it someday. The fact that time will continue after we die does not negate the time that we were alive. We are alive now, and nothing can erase that.

2

THE MEANING OF DEATH, PART ONE OF MANY

We talk a lot about the meaning of life. I want to talk for a bit about the meaning of death.

In the most straightforward literal sense, when you don't believe in God or an afterlife, there is no meaning of death. Not in any external, objective sense. In the godless universe, death just happens. It doesn't serve a purpose —there is no purpose. There's no intention behind its When and How and Why; no designer picking people off according to some mysterious master plan. Death happens because of the laws of cause and effect in the physical universe, the laws of biology and chemistry and physics. It happens because it happens.

And along with many atheists and other godless folk, I don't find this idea depressing or nihilistic. This may come as a surprise to many religious believers, but it's true. It's taken me a while to get there, but I actually find this idea rather comforting.

See, the cool thing about godlessness is that you get to create meaning. Contrary to popular opinion, a godless life isn't a life without meaning. It's a life in which we create our own meaning. Our meaning of life, of course—but also our meaning of death.

So that's what I want to talk about. Not, "What purpose does death serve for the non-existent designer?" But instead, "What meaning can death have for us? How can death shape our understanding and experience of life? What meaning of death can we create?"

And one of the things that works best for me is to see death—permanent, designerless, physical cause-and-effect death—as something that intimately connects us with the universe.

My mother died of cancer at the age of 45, when I was 17, two months after I started college. I don't talk about it much. It was terrible. It was traumatic. It was unbelievably lousy timing, mostly for her but for me as well. It was horribly unfair.

Except that it wasn't unfair. Any more than a star going nova is unfair, or a cliff collapsing into the sea.

When you don't believe that all death happens by design—the grand cosmic design of an all-powerful, all-knowing, all-good god who theoretically loves you—you don't have to torture yourself wondering what you did wrong. You don't have to twist yourself into contortions trying to figure out why you're being punished, what lesson you're supposed to learn. When people die young, when people die in terrible pain, when people die freakishly for no apparent reason, you don't have to pile onto your pain and grief any extra guilt about being punished—or any extra guilt because you're trying to see a reason for it and can't.

Instead, you can see death as part of the way the world works. We are an animal species in the physical world, and animals in the physical world get sick, or get in accidents, or get birth defects, or die in natural disasters. Sometimes good people, sometimes too young. And if it happens to you, or someone you love, it's not because you or they did something wrong. You can accept it, and grieve over it, and move on.

And when it comes to contemplating your own death, you can see it in much the same way. Death is the thing that will ultimately separate you from the universe—and yet, paradoxically, it connects you with it as well.

Death sucks, and premature death sucks worse. But it's part of the package deal of getting to be alive. It happens because you, and all the people around you, are part of the world; the physical, natural world, with all of its wonders and horrors. It's a world that doesn't really care whether you live or die, whether you suffer or rejoice, and to some people that can seem bleak and cold. But it's a world of which we are a part, a world which we are intimately connected to down to our very molecules— not a world that stands apart from us and punishes us for reasons we can never fathom.

And without a god, you don't have to figure out what purpose your death is serving. You don't have to torture yourself trying to figure out the motivations of the physical universe. It doesn't have any. So you can accept the inevitability of death, and get on with your life.

3

THE MEANING OF DEATH, PART TWO OF MANY

MOTIVATION AND MID-LIFE CRISES

When I was forty, I went through a classic mid-life crisis. No, I didn't buy a sports car or have an affair with a much younger woman. Instead, I quit a high-ranking position in a lucrative career that demanded an enormous amount of my time and energy—and took a lower-paying job, with less stress and shorter, more flexible hours, so I could concentrate on my writing.

The only thing that wasn't classic about my midlife

crisis (apart from the lack of sports cars and younger women) was how conscious it was. I wasn't deluded about it; I wasn't trying to fool myself into thinking it wasn't happening. I knew exactly what was happening. In fact, I ran with it.

What happened was that I hit forty—and realized that I didn't have an infinite amount of time to get my writing career off the ground. Of course I'd known before this that I was going to die. I'm not an idiot. But there's a difference between knowing something intellectually, and feeling it viscerally—having it shoved in your face. I hit forty, and I became aware—vividly, unignorably aware—that I was going to die someday . . . and I didn't want to be on my deathbed at seventy or eighty, wondering if I could have had a serious writing career, and regretting that I'd never really tried to make it happen.

I've been doing professional freelance writing, mostly as a sideline, since I was in my twenties. I've known for a long time that writing was what I wanted to do with my life. But it wasn't until I turned forty that I got serious about making it a priority. Not just in theory; not just the kind of "making it a priority" that involves telling everyone you know what a high priority something is for you. It became an actual priority. It became the kind of priority that involves making sacrifices. The kind of priority that means missing parties and movies and concerts because you have to spend that time working. The kind of priority that involves staying up until four in the morning to meet your deadlines, sometimes for days in a row. The kind of priority that involves taking a less demanding job for less than half your previous pay—with all the sacrifices of comfort and pleasure and security that go along with that.

And I never would have done it if I hadn't had my mid-life crisis wake-up call. I never would have done it if I hadn't started to get panicked about how little time I had left to do it.

In other words, I never would have done it without death.

I'd love to think that I'm the kind of person who would spend immortality doing marvelous things; writing novels and learning Latin, working in soup kitchens and becoming a championship ballroom dancer, reading all of Dickens and traveling to Madagascar. But I know that's bullshit. I'm the kind of person who would spend immortality sitting on the sofa eating chocolate chips and watching "Project Runway" marathons.

Heck, I'm immortal. I've got all the time in the world. I can do all that Dickens and Madagascar stuff next week. Next year. Next decade.

I'm a very deadline-driven person. And death is a deadline.

I won't lie. If I could magically be given immortality, I'd probably take it. I'd know without a doubt that it would be a terrible, unwise decision—and I'd take it anyway. The instinct to survive is too strong, too deeply-ingrained, for me to pretend otherwise. So I'm not saying that, given a choice, I'd choose death.

What I'm saying is this: Given that I don't have a choice, given that death is an unavoidable and final reality, I'm finding ways, not just to accept it, but to use it to give my life meaning. The finality of death is giving my life motivation and focus. It's driving me to accomplish things that I'd put off indefinitely without it. Death has turned me from a happy-go-lucky slacker chick with some vague creative goals but no real plans for reaching them, into an ambitious, determined woman with a clear sense of what she wants to do with her life and what she needs to do to make it happen.

And for that, I'm grateful.

4

THE MEANING OF DEATH,
PART THREE OF MANY

Sometimes, the only way through it is to just go through it.

In the face of grief and death, atheists have so much to offer. We have insights, philosophies, comforts, wisdom. But there are times when the wisest philosophies and the most thoughtful insights do nothing to alleviate our fear and grief. There are times when they don't even scratch the surface. And yet, some atheists feel guilty or bad when they feel grief, fear, or despair, to a degree that can feel inconsolable, over the finality of death. They feel like they're somehow not being good atheists, like they're letting down the team. So right now, I want to offer something a little different.

Death is natural, and we shouldn't try to pretend that it doesn't exist and isn't real.

But the fear of death, the desire not to die, the grief when people we love die, is also natural. (After all, if our species didn't have a strong preference for living over dying, we wouldn't have lasted very long.)

Death is natural—but the fear of death is also natural. And we shouldn't try to pretend that this doesn't exist, either.

I had a very good therapist once. We did a certain amount of the usual therapy stuff: talking ad nauseam to help me gain insight into my behavior and help me choose it more consciously, yada yada yada. But a lot of what we did was simply to create a safe place for me to experience emotions that I was afraid of, emotions that I kept shoving to the back burner because they felt so enormous it seemed like they were going to overwhelm me. Grief and fear over death were high on the list.

And what I found was that, sometimes—often, maybe even most of the time—the best way to deal with difficult and painful emotions is to stop trying to fix them and just let myself feel them. When I let myself actually feel my emotions, they tend to pass. Sometimes they come back, of course; but then they pass again. And when I let myself feel my emotions instead of dodging them, they're not compounded by the meta-fear, the fear of the emotion adding to whatever the emotion is that I'm afraid of.

I will caution that this "actually experiencing your grief and fear of death" thing only works if you have a pretty solid foundation to begin with. And that's where all these wonderful atheist and humanist philosophies about death come in. Such as:

The idea that loss, including death, is necessary for life and change to be possible.

The idea that death is necessary to focus our lives and make us treasure the people and experiences we have.

The idea that death is a deadline: that knowing life is temporary brings focus to our lives, inspires us to treasure the people and experiences we encounter, and motivates us to do something valuable with the short time we have.

The idea that things don't have to be permanent to be valuable and meaningful. (Many thanks go to the movie "Rivers and Tides" for getting this one across so vividly.)

The idea that death is a natural, physical process that connects us intimately with nature and the universe.

The idea that each one of us was astronomically lucky to have been born at all, and that complaining that our lives aren't infinite is like winning a million dollars in the lottery and complaining that we didn't win a hundred billion, or indeed all the money in the world.

The idea that your genes, or your ideas, will live on after you die.

The idea that your life, your slice of the timeline, will always have existed even though you die—and that even though your life has an ending as well as a beginning, that ending doesn't eradicate the time you were alive.

The idea that we didn't exist for billions of years before we were born, and that wasn't a painful or bad experience; so therefore, as frightened as we sometimes are of death, being dead won't be any different from not having been born yet.

The idea that we are free to create our own meaning of life—and our own meaning of death.

Etc., etc., etc.

None of this philosophy gives us an escape from deep fear or grief over death. Nothing gives us that. What it can give us is a solid place to come back to when the fear and grief have passed. It gives us a bridge over the chasm, a life preserver to hang on to when the fear and grief are gripping us. It gives us the strength to actually feel our fear and grief and despair—because we trust that we have a safe place to return to when the feelings pass.

And I think that, for all the comforting philosophies we can offer, the most powerful thing we can give each other in the face of death is companionship and witness. When I'm struggling with the fear of my own death, or with grief over the death of someone I love, what comforts me most isn't philosophies or ideas. It's the presence of someone who loves me just sitting with me silently, letting me feel what I have to feel, not trying to fix it or make it go away but simply being with me while I feel it. It's the presence of someone who loves me letting me know that I'm not alone—and by their presence, being part of the foundation I can come back to when the feelings pass.

I think American culture has a pathological fear

of painful emotions, and a freakish sense that they somehow make you a failure. And I know that people often feel helpless in the face of other people's grief and want desperately to fix it, to find a magic button that will make it go away. I've sat with grieving friends and felt that way myself. But I also know that there is no magic button, and that sometimes the only way out of fear and grief and despair is to just go through it.

So here's the final thing I want to say to any non-believer who's struggling with death:

Yes, I have these feelings, too. I sometimes have the despairing feeling that death eradicates and trivializes my life; the sense that, without immortality, my life is meaningless. And I also sometimes have the apparently opposite (but actually related, I think) experience; the despairing feeling that life itself is a burden, a parade of petty struggles and mundane samenesses that end only in nothingness and the void.

But I don't feel that way most of the time. Most of the time, I love my life passionately, and accept the inevitability of death with a fair amount of peace. And the fact that despair creeps in from time to time does not, I think, make me a failure as a person, or a failure as an atheist. It just makes me human.

5

LYDIA'S CANCER,
AND ATHEIST PHILOSOPHIES OF DEATH

December 6, 2010

I write a lot about atheist philosophies of death. In the last few months, I've been dealing with some of death's harsher realities. So I've been thinking a lot about how atheism, and humanism, can help us deal with death—and with life. Not just in an abstract philosophical sense; not just in a "creating a meaningful frame for our lives" sense. I've been thinking about how we can apply atheist philosophies in a practical way. I've been thinking, not just about how these philosophies can help us face death, but about how they can improve the way we live our life.

Our cat, Lydia, was recently diagnosed with cancer. Now, if you've ever had pets, you know: when they get sick or injured, or when they die, it's obviously not as serious or traumatic as when a person we love gets sick or injured or dies—but it's not trivial, either. It's a big deal.

So our cat Lydia has cancer, and it's been very difficult on both me and my wife Ingrid. And it's especially difficult because we've been having to make lots of difficult decisions, often with limited and incomplete information.

Lydia's not so sick that our decisions are all really obvious—and she's not doing so great that our decisions are all really obvious, either. She's kind of in the middle. She's been having a hard time a lot of the time, but she's been doing okay a lot of the time, and there's reasonable hope that, with treatment, the cancer will go into remission. And our information has been very incomplete. Tests on the cancer have been inconclusive, and we didn't know at first whether the cancer was a slow-growing kind that would very likely respond well to milder treatment, or a faster-growing kind that would need aggressive, difficult-to-tolerate treatment, with real uncertainty about whether it would even work. One test even suggested that she might not have cancer at all, and that the positive cancer tests might have been mistaken. As a friend who also has a sick cat put it: Rollercoaster is the new normal.

Plus, Lydia is neither a very young nor a very old cat (she's thirteen), so the questions about how much more time we can give her, balanced against how much suffering the cancer treatment will cause her, are very iffy. With or without the cancer, she could have many more years, or she could only have a few more months. And she has other medical problems, with her appetite and digestion, which have been making diagnosis and treatment harder. Are her poor appetite and weight loss a result of the cancer, or the digestion problems? Did she respond so badly to the chemo because her digestive system is so screwed up, or because she really can't tolerate it?

And all of this is making decisions about her care really, really hard. The last few months have been a parade of difficult, often wrenching choices, on an almost daily basis. Should we stop the chemo that seems to be making her sick—or keep going? Rush her to the emergency vet when her appetite drops—or keep an eye on her and see how she does? Hold off on the cancer treatment altogether until we can get the digestive stuff under control, and take the risk that the cancer will advance too far to be treatable—or pursue the cancer treatment, and take the risk that the resulting loss of appetite and weight will make her already poor health even more fragile? Pursue aggressive surgical options for the digestive problems, in the hopes that it'll make her feel better and make the cancer treatment go more smoothly—or don't put her through that trauma, since she has cancer and may not have that much time left anyway?

It's been a parade of small, difficult decisions, all framed by one very large, very difficult decision: When do we keep pursuing treatment, and when do we let go?

But there is one thing that's been making all our decisions easier.

And that's that we accept the inevitability of her death.

We understand that, someday, Lydia is going to die. If she doesn't die of the cancer in the next few months, she's going to die eventually. Of the cancer—or of something else.

Lydia is mortal. She's an animal, and all animals eventually die.

So when we've been looking at these hard decisions, we haven't been looking at them in terms of, "Is she going to live or die?" We've been looking at them in terms of, "When is she going to die?"

Does she have a few weeks, a few months, a few years?

We understand that, someday, she's going to die.

We understand that we can't make her live forever. We understand that her time here is limited, and that all we can do for her is to make that time—whether that's a few weeks, a few months, a few years—as happy as we possibly can.

So when we're making decisions about her treatment, we can look at them with frankness and clarity. We can ask questions like, "Should we give her a few months of somewhat traumatic treatment, for a decent chance at a couple/few more happy years—or should we drop it, and give her a few months of relative peace and comfort?" That's not an easy question, and the balance shifts back and forth almost every day, with new information, and with new responses to treatments, and with new developments in Lydia's own mood and health. But we can face it directly. We don't have to dance around it.

And this isn't just true about our cat.

We understand the same thing about ourselves.

We understand that we, ourselves, are going to die. We understand that our own time here is limited. We understand that all we can do for ourselves and for one another it to make that time—however much time it is—as happy and joyful and meaningful as we possibly can.

And so, when it comes time for us to face these difficult decisions about ourselves and each other, I think we'll be ready. Or as ready as you can be. If one of us gets (for instance) cancer, we'll be able to ask questions like, "Would I rather face a traumatic and horrible few months for an X% chance at a few more years—or would I rather let go and make my last few months really count?" And we'll be able to answer those questions based on a candid, hard-headed evaluation of how horrible the horribleness is likely to be, and how much time we'd probably have left even if everything went perfectly, and how much fun that time would likely be, and just how big that X% chance probably is.

We'll understand that the questions won't be, "Am I going to live or die?" We'll understand that the questions will be, "When will I die?" And we'll be able to make our decisions accordingly, with frankness and clarity.

Now, at this point, you might be wondering what any of this has to do with atheism. You might be thinking, "But religious people know that their pets are going to die! They know that the people they love are going to die! They even know that they themselves are going to die! They disagree with atheists about what happens after we die—but they know that death is real, and inevitable. What does making clear-eyed choices about death and life have to do with atheism?"

And that's a fair question.

But I've seen some research that sheds light on this question. There was a study, published in the Journal of the American Medical Association in 2009,[1] showing that, among terminally ill cancer patients, those with strong religious beliefs who relied on their religion to cope with their illness were *more* likely to get aggressive medical care in the last week of their life.

In other words: People who are most strongly attached to a belief in an afterlife are *more* likely to try to delay death when it's clearly imminent.

That doesn't make any logical sense. If people believe in a blissful afterlife, then logically, you'd think they'd accept their death gracefully, and would even welcome it. But it makes perfect sense when you think of religion, not as a way of genuinely coping with the fear of death, but as a way of putting it on the back burner.

The dominant way we deal with death in our culture is religious. And our religious culture deals with death by pretending it isn't real. Religion deals with death by pretending it isn't permanent; by pretending that the loss of the ones we love is just like a long vacation apart; by pretending that our dead loved ones are still hanging around somehow, like the dead grandparents in a "Family Circus" cartoon; by pretending that our own death is just a one-way trip to a different place. Our religious culture deals with death by putting it on the back burner, by encouraging people to stick their fingers in their ears and yell, "I can't hear you, I can't hear you, I can't hear you!" (This is backed up, again, by the JAMA study,[2] which also showed that a high level of religious coping was associated with less use of end-of-life planning strategies, including do-not-resuscitate orders, living wills, and appointment of a health care power of attorney.)

So when religious people are faced with the harsh realities of death—and with the possibility that their beliefs might be bogus and that death might really, truly be the end—they're often not prepared. They haven't had to think about the inevitability of death, and its finality, and what kinds of choices they would make when faced with it.

Hence, the lack of practical preparation for death—and the pointlessly aggressive medical care in the last week of life.

Atheists, on the other hand, have *had* to come up with ways of dealing with death, more or less on our own. Like anyone who rejects the dominant culture, and who rejects the default answers to hard questions that get spoon-fed to us by this culture, we've had to come up with our own answers. The same way that LGBT people are forced to think about sexuality and gender; the same way that vegetarians are forced to think about the ethics of food . . . atheists are forced to think about death, and what kind of value life might have when it's brief and finite. If we once had religious beliefs about an immortal afterlife, letting go of those beliefs forced us to think about death, and to face its finality, and to come up with ways of coping with it. And even if we were raised non-believers, the religious views of death are so ubiquitous in our culture that they're impossible to ignore—and non-religious alternatives, to put it mildly, aren't. They are the exact opposite of ubiquitous. Atheists have had to come up with these alternatives more or less on our own. (To be fair, some religious adherents have thought carefully about these questions too, the way some straight people and cisgendered people and carnivores have thought carefully about sexuality and gender and food ethics — but being an atheist means having that thoughtfulness thrust upon us, whether we like it or not.)

So when the subject of death arises, atheists can't evade it. We can't paper it over with a Band-Aid of "Well, we'll see each other again on the other side," with no careful thought about whether that other side is remotely plausible, or whether it would be desirable even if it existed. And every time we hear people talk about Heaven or angels or past lives or their loved ones being in a better place and looking down on them right now, we're reminded: "Oh, yeah. We don't think that. We think that when we die, we die forever. We don't think our dead loved ones are with God. We think that they're fucking dead." We have to face death a little bit, every day of our lives.

It's like an inoculation.

So when it comes time to face death for real, we're ready. Of course we're frightened by it; of course we're upset by it; of course we want to delay it if we reasonably can, for as long as we reasonably can. Life is precious, and of course we grieve for its end. But it doesn't take us by surprise—not in the same way that it does for believers. We've had time to think about it. We've had time to think about questions like quantity of life versus quality of life, and how these balance out for us. We've had time to think about questions like what makes life meaningful even though it's finite—and how to make that meaning still be meaningful, even when that finiteness is looking very finite indeed.

And so when our pets get sick, or when our parents start to get frail, or when we're facing hard decisions about our own life and death—we're not caught off-guard. We can make informed, evidence-based choices that are in keeping with our deepest and most treasured values, and that aren't just frightened, reflexive reactions to the single undeniable reality of our life.

When people with life-threatening illnesses like cancer or HIV are given a good prognosis, they're sometimes told, "You'll live long enough to die of something else." That may sound grisly and morbid to some. But to me, it's oddly comforting. It offers the comfort of the solid foundation of reality. It offers the comfort of understanding that yes, we're going to die someday—and so, armed with that understanding, we can make good, thoughtful choices about our death, and about our life.

If you're a believer who's questioning your beliefs, leaving your religion does mean facing the finality and permanence of death. That can be a hard pill to swallow. But when I think about those religious believers frantically pursuing aggressive and pointless medical care in the last week of their lives . . . it seems like a bargain.

Postscript: Lydia died on December 26, 2010.

Notes

1. Andrea C. Phelps, MD et al., "Religious Coping and Use of Intensive Life-Prolonging Care Near Death in Patients With Advanced Cancer," *Journal of the American Medical Association*, March 18, 2009, http://jama.jamanetwork.com/article.aspx?articleid=183578.

2. Phelps, "Religious Coping."

6

DO WE CONCEDE THE GROUND
OF DEATH TOO EASILY?

"Sure, atheism may have better arguments and evidence. But religion is always to going to win on the death question. A secular philosophy of death will never comfort people the way religion does."

I've heard this idea more times than I can count. And here's the weird thing: It's not just from religious believers. I hear it from some atheists, too. It shocks me how easily many non-believers concede the ground of death. Many of us assume that of course it would be lovely to believe in an eternal afterlife—if only that were plausible.

And largely because of this assumption, we often

shy away from the topic of death. We happily talk about science, sex, reality, medicine and technology, other advantages the secular life has to offer—but we stay away from death, and concede the ground before we even fight it.

I think this is a huge mistake. I agree that the fear of death is one of the main reasons people cling to religion. But I don't agree, even in the slightest, that religious philosophies of death are inherently more comforting than secular ones. And if we want to make atheism a safe place to land when people let go of their faith, we need to get these secular philosophies into the public square, and let the world know what we think about death.

Here's the thing you have to remember about religious beliefs in an afterlife: They're only comforting if you don't examine them.

Heaven is the most obvious example. The idea of a perfect, blissful afterlife where you and everyone you love will live forever . . . think about it for a moment. All your conflicts with the people you care about—do those just disappear? If they don't, how will Heaven be perfectly blissful? And if they do disappear, how will you be you? Conflicts arise because people are individuals, with real differences between us. In Heaven, either those conflicts will still be raging, or our differences—the individuality that makes us who we are—will be eradicated.

Then ask yourself this: In Heaven, would we have the ability to do harm, or to make bad decisions? Again—if we do, it won't be perfect or blissful. But if we don't, we've lost one of the essential things that makes us who we are. Even Christians understand this: they're always going on about how free will makes us special, how it's a unique gift God gave to humanity, how God had to make us free to do evil so we could choose to do good. Yet when we're in Heaven, when we're in the perfect place that God created for us to be our most perfect selves . . . this unique gift, the gift that's the sole reason for suffering and evil, somehow vanishes into thin air?

And when you're in Heaven, will you remember the people who didn't make it? Will you be aware of your loved ones—or anyone, for that matter—screaming and begging for mercy in the eternal agony of Hell? Again: If you are aware of this torture, there is no way for Heaven to be blissful, even for a microsecond. But if you're not—if you're so blissed-out by God's presence that your awareness of Hell is obliterated, like morphine obliterating your awareness of pain—how could you be you? Isn't our love and compassion for others one of the best, most central parts of who we are? How could we possibly be who we are, and not care about the suffering of the people we love?

This is not abstract philosophizing. This question of how Heaven will be Heaven if our loved ones are burning in Hell . . . it's a question many Christians struggle with terribly. My wife's fundamentalist grandparents were tormented because their children and grandchildren had all left the church, and they were sure they were all going to burn. It created deep strife in her family, and caused her grandparents great unhappiness in their old age. And the monstrous notion of being so blissed-out in Heaven you won't notice your loved ones shrieking for mercy in Hell . . . this is put forward by many Christian theologians, including the supposedly respectable William Lane Craig, in response to direct questions from believers who find this whole "not knowing or caring if our loved ones are in agony" thing rather hard to swallow.

And I haven't even gotten to the monotony of Heaven. I haven't even started on how people need change, challenges, growth, to be happy, and how an eternity of any one thing would eventually become tedious to the point of madness. Unless, again, our personalities changed so much we'd be unrecognizable.

I'm with Christopher Hitchens on this one. Heaven

sounds like North Korea—an eternity of mindless conformity spent singing the praises of a powerful tyrant. In order for it to actually be perfect and blissful, our natures would have to change so radically, we wouldn't be who we are. The idea is comforting only if you think about it for a fleeting moment —"Oo, eternal bliss and seeing everyone I love forever!"—and you then immediately shove it to the back of your mind and start thinking about something else.

The same is true for every other afterlife I've heard of. Reincarnation, for instance. If dying and being reborn obliterates the memories of our past lives . . . then without those memories, how would we be ourselves? And it's true of the notion of our souls being dissolved into the soup of a larger World-Soul: nice idea, maybe, but how is it immortality if our unique identity is gone? I have never heard of any imagined afterlife that could withstand more than a few minutes of careful examination without sounding like a nightmare.

This is conspicuously not true with secular philosophies of death.

Secular philosophies of death—that being dead will be no more frightening than not yet being born, that death helps us focus and acts as a deadline, that permanence isn't the only measure of value, any of the others—can withstand scrutiny. They can withstand scrutiny, because they're based in reality. (Most of them, anyway. There are secular notions of death that I think are self-deluded, but they're the exception, not the rule.)

And for many atheists, this is a profound comfort.

When I was a spiritual believer, thinking about death meant being propelled into cognitive dissonance. I'd think, "Oh, my mom's not really dead, my friend Rob isn't really dead, I'm not really going to die"—and then I'd get uncomfortable, and anxious, and I'd have to think about something else right away. On some level, I knew that my spiritual beliefs didn't make sense, that they weren't supported by good evidence, that they were mostly founded on wishful thinking, that I was making them up as I went along. I was comforted by them only to the degree that I didn't think about them.

And that's not a happy way to live.

When I finally did let go of my wishful thinking, I went through a traumatic time. I had to accept that I was never going to see my mother again, or my friend Rob, and that when I died I would really be gone forever. That was intensely hard. But once I started building a new, secular foundation for dealing with death, I found it far more consoling. I wasn't constantly juggling a flock of inconsistent, incoherent ideas—or shoving them onto the back burner. When I was grieving the death of someone I loved, or when I was frightened by my own eventual death, I could actually, you know, think about my ideas. I could actually feel my feelings. I could actually experience my grief, and my fear—because my understanding of death was based on reality, and could withstand as much exploration as I cared to give it. The comfort I've gotten from my humanist philosophy hasn't been as easy or simple as the comfort I once got from my belief in a world-soul and a reincarnated afterlife—but it's been a whole lot more solid.

And I'm not the only one that's true for. I've talked with lots of non-believers about this, and I've lost count of the number who've said something like, "Yeah, eternity seems like a good idea, but once I started thinking about it, I realized it would suck. Dealing with death as an atheist seems like it'd be harsh—but actually, I find it easier."

This is a subjective question, of course. If you, personally, don't find secular philosophies of death comforting or appealing, then you don't. But . . . well, actually, that's my point. It's absurd to say that religious ideas about death are inherently more appealing than secular ones. For a lot of us, they aren't. For a lot of us, the exact opposite is true.

So let's stop treating death as if it belongs to religion.

We don't have to be afraid of this topic. We can talk about it. And we should talk about it. There are many believers who feel the way I used to: they're having questions, they're having doubts, but they're scared to let go. They're scared to imagine a life where death is real, and final. If we can get our ideas and feelings about death out into the world, these people will find it easier to let go—knowing they'll have a safe place to land when they do.

When it comes to death, we don't have to simply say, "Of course religion is a comforting lie—but it's still a lie, and you should care about that." For many people, the lie is not actually very comforting. And the very fact that it is a lie is a large part of what undercuts its comfort.

We do not have to concede this ground.

7

ATHEISM, DEATH, AND THE DIFFERENCE BETWEEN PESSIMISM AND REALISM

What is an appropriate atheist philosophy of death?

And how should atheists be talking about death with believers?

I once did a writing project, the Atheist Meme of the Day, in which I wrote pithy memes briefly explaining one aspect of atheism or exploding one myth about it, and asking people to pass them on if they liked.

Some of my Memes generated disagreement from some atheists. Which was fine, of course. But the ones that generated the most vigorous pushback surprised me. Consistently, they were the ones about death: the ones trying to show that a godless view of death can offer some solace and meaning; the ones that began, "Atheism does have comfort to offer in the face of death."

Whenever I wrote one of these, I could almost guarantee that within a few hours—usually within a few minutes—some atheist would be complaining that the comforting philosophy I was presenting wasn't comforting at all. Some atheists even claimed that it was literally impossible for an atheist philosophy of death to offer anything even comparable to the comfort offered by religion. They argued that it was either deceptive or deluded, a denial of reality, to pretend that this was possible, and that we shouldn't even try. This wasn't the majority response, but it wasn't rare, either.

I'm baffled by this. To say the least. So I want to examine why there's resistance, from atheists, to the very idea of presenting atheist philosophies of death that give comfort, meaning, and hope. And I want to explain what exactly I mean by "comforting atheist ideas about death."

I think part of the problem here may lie with the word "comfort"—and with some people's expectations of it. So let me explain what I mean by that.

When I say that some particular view of death offers

comfort, I don't mean that it completely eradicates any pain or grief associated with death. Of course it doesn't. Nothing does that—not even religion. (More on that in a moment.) When I say, "This view of death offers some comfort," I'm not saying, "If you look at death this way, it will no longer trouble you. With this philosophy, you can view death blithely, even cheerfully. The death of the ones you love, and your own eventual death, will no longer suck even in the slightest."

That's not what I mean by "comfort."

When I say, "This atheist philosophy of death offers comfort," I mean, "This atheist philosophy can, to some extent, alleviate the suffering and grief caused by death. It can make the suffering and grief feel less overwhelming, less unbearable. It doesn't make the pain disappear—but it can put the experience into a context that gives it some sort of meaning, and it can offer the hope that with time, the pain will diminish. It can give us a sense that there's a bridge over the chasm; a feeling of trust that, when the worst of the grief passes, we'll have a solid foundation to return to. It doesn't make the grief or fear go away—but it can lighten the load."

That's what I mean by "comfort." It would be nice if an atheist philosophy of death could do more: but given how monumentally frightening and upsetting death is, the fact that atheism can provide even this degree of comfort is not trivial.

And maybe more to the point: Religion doesn't do any better.

Ever since I became an atheist, I've been struck by the fact that, even when people believe that death is no more than a temporary separation, they still grieve, deeply and desperately, for the people they love, as if they were never going to see those people again. Belief in an afterlife doesn't keep people from mourning in terrible anguish when their loved ones die. It doesn't keep people from missing the loved ones they've lost, and missing them for years, missing them for the rest of their lives. And it doesn't keep people from fearing their own death, and putting it off as long as they can. (And for the record: No, I don't think this makes them hypocrites. I think it makes them human.) The comfort of religion doesn't eradicate grief, any more than the comfort of atheism does. It simply alleviates it to some extent.

But does an atheist philosophy of death offer *less* comfort than a religious one? Honestly—I think that depends. For one thing, it depends on the atheist philosophy. A philosophy of (to give one example) "Yes, I'm going to die, but my ideas and the effect I had on the world will live on for a while " will probably be more comforting than a philosophy of, "Yeah, death sucks, but that's reality, reality bites, whaddya gonna do."

Plus, obviously, it depends on the religion as well. Many true believers in a blissful afterlife aren't actually very comforted by their belief. It's common for believers to be tormented by the thought that, even though they're going to Heaven, the apostates in their family are going to burn in Hell—and how can Heaven be Heaven if their loved ones are burning in Hell? And many religious beliefs about death fill their believers, not with comfort, but with terror and guilt—and many atheists who once held those beliefs say that letting go of them was a profound relief. They would much rather believe in no afterlife at all than an afterlife governed by the vengeful, nitpicky, capricious, psychopathically sadistic god they were brought up to believe in.

And whether atheism or religion offers more comfort in the face of death depends an awful lot on the person. When I believed in an afterlife, I always had a nagging, uncomfortable feeling in the back of my mind that my beliefs weren't based on anything substantial, that they weren't sincere beliefs so much as wishful thinking. Compared to my current conclusions—that when we die, our consciousness will disappear entirely—I suppose those beliefs were more comforting. Or they would have been, if it hadn't been for my uneasy suspicion that they were bullshit. But . . . well, that's my point. My current ways of coping with death offer a major source of comfort that my old beliefs couldn't give me, a source of comfort that more than compensates for the false hope of immortality. And that's a strong degree of confidence that I'm not deluding myself. As Ayaan Hirsi Ali wrote: "The only position that leaves me with no cognitive dissonance is atheism." Having no cognitive dissonance in my philosophy of death is a profound comfort. This might not be true for everybody: some people do seem better able to live with cognitive dissonance than others. But it's certainly true for me. And it seems to be true for many other people.

Which brings me back to my point:

Yes, I care about reality. Any regular reader of my writing knows that I care about reality to an almost obsessive degree. I am not a fan of pretty lies that make people feel better (with the exception of certain social niceties, like "Your baby is beautiful" and "I liked your poem"), and the argument that "it doesn't matter whether religion is really true" fills me with sputtering rage. I think reality is far more important than anything we could make up about it—pretty much by definition.

But it is not a denial of reality to offer comforting

thoughts about death that have nothing to do with God.

It bugs me when atheists with a more bleak view of death than mine present that bleakness as a logical consequence of atheism, the inherent result of not believing in God or an afterlife. It bugs me partly because I disagree, obviously. But it also bugs me because it treats a question of personal opinion as if it were a question of fact.

Look. Questions like, "Is there a god?" "Is there a soul?" "Is there an afterlife?"—these are questions of fact, questions we can and should be debating the evidence for. But questions like, "Is it comforting to view death as a natural process, something that connects us with the great chain of cause and effect in the universe?" or, "Is it comforting to view death as a deadline, something we need to inspire us to accomplish anything?"—these are questions of subjective opinion, personal perspective. We can discuss and debate them—but ultimately, they are questions that can be legitimately answered with, "If it's true for me, then it's true for me." If it comforts people, then it comforts people. So it bugs me when atheists argue that these forms of comfort are delusional—because it treats a personal perspective on life as if it were a question of fact.

And when it comes to questions of perspective and

opinion and personal philosophy—why *not* try to be positive? Why *not* try to frame our experience in ways that are hopeful and meaningful and comforting? And why not share those ways of framing experience with people who are considering atheism but are scared to pieces about it? Of course our philosophies should be consistent with reality—but if we have a choice in different ways of dealing with that reality, why not choose the ones that minimize suffering and maximize joy?

I'm not trying to pretend that death doesn't suck. I'm not trying to pretend that the finality of death with no afterlife doesn't suck. Death sucks—and it should. Life is precious, and we should treasure it, and mourn its loss. If we care about the people we love, it is reasonable and right to grieve when they die: if we care about our own self and our own life, it is reasonable and right to grieve in advance for the eventual end of that life.

But we can find ways to frame reality—including the reality of death—that make it easier to deal with. We can find ways to frame reality that do not ignore or deny it, and that still give us comfort and solace, meaning and hope. And we can offer these ways of framing reality to people who are considering atheism but have been taught to see it as terrifying, empty, and hopeless.

And I'm genuinely baffled by atheists who are trying

to undercut that. It's not like I'm not pulling these ideas out of my ass: every meme I've written about death has been a view that some atheists I know of find comforting. There's a difference between saying, "Gee, that isn't my experience, I don't find that idea comforting"—and saying, "You shouldn't find it comforting, either. Nobody should find it comforting. Death still sucks even when you look at it that way—therefore, that view isn't comforting at all, to anyone. There is no way atheism can ever offer a philosophy of death that will be as comforting as religion. That's just an objective fact. We shouldn't even try." I am baffled by people who so vehemently insist on this bleak response—not just for themselves, but for everyone.

There were a lot of things I was trying to do with these Atheist Memes of the Day in particular, and that I'm trying to do with my atheist writing in general. (All the memes and all the writing—not just the stuff about death.) I'm trying to dispel misconceptions and bigotries about atheism. I'm trying to disseminate methods of critical thinking, about religion specifically and reality generally. I'm trying to get people to view religion as just another idea about how the world works, with no more right to special treatment than any other idea.

But one of the biggest things I'm trying to do is to help make atheism a safe place to land. I'm trying to make the world a safer place to be an atheist; not just safer from the bigotry and hostility of others, but safer emotionally and psychologically for the people who are considering it. The journey out of religion and into atheism can be a frightening and traumatic one, even under the best of circumstances. And the fear of the permanence of death is often one of the most frightening and traumatic parts of that transition.

I'm trying to help ease that transition. I'm trying to show that an atheist life can be good and happy and joyful, and that, while losing religion will often mean losing some forms of comfort and meaning, there will be new forms of comfort and meaning to replace them— including new ways of dealing with death. The world is increasingly full of people who are falling out of religion, or who are close to falling out of it. I'm trying to help create a safety net, to make that landing softer.

And I'm genuinely baffled when it seems like other atheists are trying to cut the ropes.

8

GRIEF BEYOND BELIEF

HOW ATHEISTS ARE DEALING WITH DEATH

How do you deal with death—your own, or that of people you love—when you don't believe in God or an afterlife?

Especially when our culture so commonly handles grief with religion—in ways that are so deeply ingrained, people often aren't aware of it?

An online faith-free grief support group, Grief Beyond Belief, is grappling with that very question. Grief Beyond Belief was launched by my friend Rebecca Hensler after the death of her three-month-old son. Shortly after Jude's death, she discovered Compassionate Friends, an extensive online network created for all parents grieving the deaths of their children. But even though Compassionate Friends is not a religious organization, she says, "I often felt alienated by assurances from other members that my son was in heaven or by offers to pray for me, comforts that were kindly meant but that I do not believe and cannot accept." And she knew there were others who felt the same way.

So about a year later, she started an online support group, Grief Beyond Belief. The group was created for atheists, agnostics, humanists, and anyone without belief in a higher power or an afterlife, to share memories, photos, thoughts, feelings or questions, and to give others support, perspective, empathy, or simply a non-judgmental ear. And it flourished—far beyond her expectations. News about it spread like wildfire, through the atheist community and outside of it; membership grew rapidly; and the group is going strong, and continuing to grow.

So why do so many atheists need and want a separate godless sub-culture—for grief support, or anything else? Why do atheists need this?

Salt in the Wound

For some grieving non-believers, the comforts offered by religious believers are neutral, and can even be positive.

These atheists don't agree that their dead loved ones are still alive and that they'll see them again someday: but they can accept the intent behind the sentiments, and can feel connected with and supported by believers even though they don't share the beliefs.

But for many non-believers, these comforts are actively upsetting. They are the antithesis of comforting. They rub salt in the wound.

For many grieving non-believers, the "comforts" of religion and religious views of death present a terrible choice: Either pretend to agree with ideas they reject and in many cases actively oppose—or open up about their non-belief, and start a potentially divisive argument at a time when they most need connection and comfort. As Grief Beyond Belief member William Farlin Cain said, "I was still very much in the atheist closet at the time [my mom] passed away, and I was surrounded by believers saying all the things believers say, and I had to say them too just to keep the peace. It was hard."

Religious ideas about death can also make atheists feel alienated—hyper-aware of their marginalized status, and of the ways that atheists in our culture are invisible at best. As I myself have told believers who were pressing their religious "comforts" on me even though I'd explicitly said I didn't want that: If you wouldn't tell a Jewish person that their dead loved one is in the arms of Jesus Christ, why would you think it's appropriate to tell a non-believer that their dead loved one is in Heaven? And yet many believers do think this is appropriate—to the point where they not only offer nonbelievers the "comfort" of their opinion that death is not final, but persist in doing so even when specifically asked not to. They're so steeped in the idea of religion as a comfort, they seem unable to think of any other way to comfort those in need. And they seem unable to see that their beliefs aren't universally shared by everyone.

But these beliefs aren't universally shared. And they aren't seen as universally comforting, either. In fact, religious ideas about death can be profoundly upsetting to people who don't believe them. Sentiments that many believers find comforting—such as Heaven and Hell, or God's plan for life and death—are, for many non-believers, more than just ideas they don't agree with. They are ideas they find distressing, hurtful, and repugnant. As Grief Beyond Belief member Lisa M. Lilly said, "After my parents were killed by a drunk driver, people said things to me that I found extremely difficult to hear, such as that their deaths were God's plan or God's will. While I'm sure the speakers thought they were offering comfort, the idea that God wanted my mother to be run over and die in the street and my father to suffer 6 1/2 weeks with severe injuries, only to die after several surgeries, was appalling to me." And as Grief Beyond Belief member Karen Vidrine commented, "Even when believers don't say it, I know they are thinking of Hell and how to tell me my children [who committed suicide] are there." Even though atheists don't agree with these ideas, they're still disturbing—and they're the last thing they want to hear about when they're struggling with their grief.

This isn't just true for non-believers, either. It's often true for grieving believers as well. In fact, as Hensler points out, the death of a loved one is often a trigger for questioning or abandoning religious faith—especially if that death is particularly painful or unjust. (This is a big reason why Hensler created the group to welcome not only atheists, but believers who are questioning their faith.) The idea that death is part of God's plan, for instance, is comforting to some—but for many, this idea either makes them angry at God, or guilt-ridden about what they or their loved ones did wrong to bring on his wrath. And the idea of Heaven or another perfectly blissful afterlife is often comforting only when you don't think about it very carefully. When you consider the idea of a spiritual "place" where we somehow are ourselves and yet magically don't change or grow, don't experience any conflict, don't have the freedom to screw up, and are untroubled by the suffering of others (either living or in Hell) . . . this idea can become more and more disturbing the more carefully you consider it. And many people find that they cope with death and grief far better without it.

But the reality is that spiritual beliefs permeate grief support—so much so that it's invisible to believers, who often perpetuate it without even thinking. As Grief Beyond Belief founder Hensler pointed out, even in the non-religious Compassionate Friends group, "so many of their members are religious or spiritual that there is no real way to participate without being constantly exposed to comments about god, angels and signs. And when I posted about my son and my grief on the page, commenters frequently projected those beliefs onto me, with offers to pray or reassurances that Jude is in heaven. Half the time I felt understood and supported, and half the time I felt like screaming." Grief Beyond Belief member Kevin Millham echoes this sentiment. "The hospice in which my wife died has a wonderful bereavement program, and I now belong to a grief support [group] there. Everyone tries to be supportive and not proselytize, but the other members are Christians without exception, and we often hear in group meetings how their faith is helping them get through (though I notice they're having every bit as hard a time as I am . . .). What helps them does not help me, however, and I find that talk of an afterlife I do not believe in is a way of minimizing my attempts to deal with the finality of my wife's death, however well-intentioned the 'better place' comments may be."

And planning funerals and memorials with religious content is so common that, even when non-believers explicitly request secular ceremonies upon their death, these wishes frequently get ignored. Said Grief Beyond Belief member Julie Downing Wirtz, "When my mom died, she left explicit instructions for her funeral. It was to be in the funeral home, not the church, she wanted 2 songs played, and she named them clearly. Well, some of my siblings chose not to honor her wishes, went to the Catholic church my mother no longer attended, somehow got the pastor there to allow the funeral service, but he would not allow the songs that my mom felt would give us comfort, since they were not religious songs." This also happened to Grief Beyond Belief member Kevin Millham when his wife died: "The memorials we had discussed and agreed upon before her death were pretty much hijacked by local religious and spiritual types."

Even supposedly secular memorials often get infused with religious or spiritual content. And this tendency is so deeply ingrained, the people planning these events aren't even aware that the content is religious, and that it might be unwelcome to non-believers. Hensler tells the story of a memorial held for a number of children, including her son—a memorial that was explicitly described as non-religious. "A book was read to all the children in attendance," she says, "who were mostly grieving siblings. The book was written from the point of view of a dead child, describing 'where I am now' in vague, stars-and-rainbows sorts of terms. It disturbed me, particularly because my late son was one of the children honored at the ceremony. How can they say an event will be non-religious and then teach the children who attend about a version of afterlife?" And before you ask—this didn't happen in a small town in the Midwest, or the deeply religious South. It happened in San Francisco— one of the most secular, least traditionally religious, most diversity-supportive cities in the country. As Hensler noted, "A whole lot of people seem to think that as long as you aren't talking about Jesus, any support you provide is universally welcome."

This latter point cannot be emphasized enough. There's an all-too-common assumption that "non-religious" means "not adhering to the tenets of a specific religious sect." If you aren't talking about Jesus, or Allah, or reincarnation—if all you're talking about is non-specific ideas of some sort of higher power or some sort of afterlife—that's typically seen to be "non-religious." Atheism—or indeed, any sort of non-belief in supernatural beings or forces—is still so invisible in our culture that the possibility simply isn't considered. So even supposedly inclusive, secular events end up with religious or spiritual content that leaves non-believers out in the cold.

But even if none of this were the case—even if grieving atheists were never confronted with religious ideas about death in upsetting or alienating ways, or even if no atheists were upset or alienated by these ideas—the need for non-faith-based grief support would still be powerful. In a time of grief, the need for others who understand, others with a similar outlook on life and death, is intense.

Secular and religious views of life—and death—can be radically different. The view that life and death are deliberately guided by a conscious supernatural being is radically different from the view that life and death are entirely natural processes, guided by physical cause and effect. The view that consciousness is a metaphysical substance with the ability to survive death is radically different from the view that consciousness is a biological process created by the brain, and that it ends when the brain dies. The view that life is permanent is radically different from the view that life is ephemeral.

And the forms of comfort and perspective that we find helpful in grief can also be radically different. The idea that life is eternal and we'll see our loved ones again someday is radically different from the idea that life is transitory and therefore ought to be intensely treasured. The idea that life and death are part of God's benevolent plan is radically different from the idea that life and death are part of natural cause and effect, and that we and our loved ones are part of the physical universe and are intimately connected with it. The idea that our dead loved ones are no longer suffering because they're in a blissful Heaven is radically different from the idea that our dead loved ones are no longer suffering because they no longer exist, and that being dead is no more painful or frightening than not having been born yet. The idea that death is an illusion is radically different from the idea that death is necessary for life and change to be possible. The idea that the soul will live forever is radically different from the idea that things don't have to be permanent to be valuable. The idea that there will be a final judgment in which the bad are punished and the good are rewarded is radically different from the idea that we were all phenomenally, astronomically lucky to have been born at all. The idea that our loved ones will always live on in an afterlife is radically different from the idea that we keep our loved ones alive in our memories, and that they live on in the ways they changed us and the world. Believers and non-believers have many things in common, and much of what we find comforting during grief is the same—but much of it is seriously different, and even contradictory.

So for many grieving non-believers, the comfort offered by religious believers is, at best, not particularly comforting. Even if it isn't actively upsetting, it simply doesn't connect. And so the comfort, perspective, practical guidance, support, and simple "I've been there and know what you're going through" empathy offered by the Grief Beyond Belief network has been intensely welcomed. As Hensler says, "One of the hardest parts about the first few days of Grief Beyond Belief was the number of people who said, "I wish this had existed when . . ."

Grief Beyond Belief member Nita-Jane Grigson: "I get a sense of support from other people going through what I'm going through, that my friends don't understand." Grief Beyond Belief member William Farlin Cain: "Other grief groups more or less insist I indulge my 'spiritual side,' and I just want something of the rational as I revisit the grieving process these years later." Grief Beyond Belief member Karen Vidrine: "I like being able to comment and vent about my children's deaths, suicides, without fear of judgment." Grief Beyond Belief member James Sweet: "I look for the same things I think just about anyone is looking for in a grief support group: To know other people are going through the same things; to vent; to share; to find hope in loss, to see that no matter how terrible the tragedy, life still goes on. I just don't need to worry so much about having to bite my tongue." Grief Beyond Belief member Lisa M. Lilly: "I am grateful to Grief Beyond Belief for providing a forum where feelings of loss are acknowledged and shared without anyone insisting that somehow the tragedy is a good thing or fits with religious views held by others." Grief Beyond Belief member Kevin Millham: "I come here to be with kindred spirits who will understand what it is I'm going through even if we do not often respond directly to each other's posts. Just knowing that I'm not alone in my (lack of) beliefs is a comfort when in my hometown I feel so alienated."

Even people who currently aren't grieving are finding Grief Beyond Belief valuable—because it helps them support the bereaved non-believers in their lives. Grief Beyond Belief member Julie Downing Wirtz says, "As a trained Funeral Celebrant, and Life Tribute Specialist, serving only non-religious families, I find the posts at

Grief Beyond Belief help me to serve my clients with a better understanding of the various thoughts that go through people's minds when they are grieving, many of which are very different from my own experiences." And Grief Beyond Belief member Christine M. Pedro-Panuyas concurs. "I haven't lost anyone close to me, but what Grief Beyond Belief has really done for me is it helped me know what to say to those who have lost someone. It helped me learn the words to say that are comforting and are comforting in a powerful way because they are true."

When The Trump Card Fails

It's commonly assumed that death is religion's trump card. No matter what atheism has to offer—a better sex life, freedom from religion's often random taboos, the embrace of reality over wishful thinking, etc.—many people automatically assume that, when it comes to death and grief, the comfort of believing in an afterlife will always win out. They assume that any argument for atheism being, you know, true, will ultimately crumble in the face of our desire for death to not be the end.

Many atheists reject this assumption passionately. We point out that many religious beliefs about death are far from comforting—Hell being the most obvious—and that many former believers welcome atheism as a profound relief. We point out that religious beliefs about death are only comforting when you don't think about them very carefully. We point out that a philosophy that accepts reality is inherently more comforting than a philosophy based on wishful thinking—since it doesn't involve cognitive dissonance and the unease of self-deception. And we point out that there are many godless philosophies of death that offer comfort, meaning, and hope—with complete acceptance of the permanence of death, and without any belief in any sort of afterlife.

But it's one thing to face the general idea of death with a godless philosophy. It's another thing entirely when someone you love dies, and you're dealing with the immediate and painful reality of grief.

And that's what groups like Grief Beyond Belief are about.

That's what the burgeoning atheist community is about.

So if you ever wonder why atheists need our own space—our own meetups, our own student groups, our own parenting groups, our own online forums, our own organizations, our own support networks—remember that.

And if you need it yourself—please know that it's here.

9

ATHEISTS IN FOXHOLES

"Sure, you deny God now. But when you're looking death in the face—when you're sick or in an accident or staring down the barrel of a gun—you'll change your mind. You'll beg for God then. There are no atheists in foxholes."

This is one of the most common accusations that gets leveled against atheists. The idea seems to be that our atheism isn't sincere. It's naive at best, shallow at worst. We haven't really thought through what atheism means: it's somehow never occurred to us that atheism—and its philosophical companion, naturalism—means that death is forever. As soon as the harsh reality of what atheism means gets shoved in our faces, we'll drop it like a hot potato.

Now, the most common atheist response to this accusation is to point out that it's simply and flatly not true. And it's one of the arguments I'm going to make myself, right now. This accusation is simply and flatly not true. If you go to an atheist blog or forum, and you make this accusation, you'll be inundated with stories of atheists who have faced death; their own, and that of people they love. You'll hear stories of people who have been mugged, people who have been in terrible accidents, people who have faced life-threatening illnesses. You'll hear stories of people who have suffered the illness and death of dearly beloved friends and family members. I'm one of those people. And we didn't stop being atheists.

This is even true of people who face death professionally, on a regular basis. Contrary to the common canard, there are, in fact, atheists in foxholes. There are atheist soldiers; atheist police officers; atheist firefighters. There are entire organizations of them. (For a while, there was actually a group of military atheists with the waggish name, "Atheists In Foxholes.")

Atheist responses to death and imminent death vary, of course, what with us being human and all. Some of us feel a desire to return to religion, a wish that we could believe in God and the afterlife and take comfort from that belief. Others of us are even more confirmed in our atheism than before; finding little comfort in the idea that death and tragedy were created deliberately by the hand of God, and finding great comfort in our humanist philosophies of life and death. But deathbed or foxhole conversions to religion are really pretty rare. (If you've heard stories about them—know that many of these stories are made up by religious believers to bolster their case.)

When you think about it, this whole argument is completely absurd. Do people really think that, out of the millions of atheists in the United States and around the world, none of us have ever been deathly ill, or suffered the loss of someone we loved? Does that even make sense?

But let's move on. Let's pretend, for the sake of argument, that this accusation is true. Let's suppose that every single atheist who's ever faced death has converted to religion.

How would that be an argument for religion being true?

If anything, it's the opposite. It's been clearly demonstrated that when we're strongly motivated to believe something, we're much more likely to believe it: we amplify the importance of evidence that seems to support this belief, filter out evidence that contradicts it, etc. When we really, really want to believe something, that's when we have to be extra-cautious about concluding that it's true—since the chances that we're just trying to talk ourselves into it have shot through the roof. The human mind's capacity to persuade itself of things it wants to believe is damn near limitless.

And the desire to believe in immortality is the mother of all wishful thinking. Especially when we're immediately confronted by death.

So if atheists only converted to religion when they were on their deathbed . . . that wouldn't be an argument for religion being a true and accurate perception of something in the real world. That'd actually be a strong argument for religion just being something people made up to make themselves feel better.

Okay. Those are the most common, most obvious defenses against the "atheists in foxholes" accusation. But I want to add something more—something that often gets left out of the conversation about foxholes and deathbed conversions.

I want to point out what an ugly argument this is.

What would you think if someone made this argument to a person of a different faith? "Sure, you believe in Judaism now—but when your plane is going down, then you'll turn to your Lord and Savior Jesus Christ"? Would you think that was an appropriate thing to say? Or would you think it was religious bigotry, pure and simple? Regardless of what you personally believe about Jesus Christ and his ability to comfort people during plane crashes ... would you think that was an appropriate thing to say? Or would you denounce it as insensitive and tone-deaf at best, callous and inhumane at worst?

So how it is any different to make this argument to atheists?

And the whole trope about "You'll change your tune when you're looking death in the face" has a Schadenfreude quality to it that is truly ugly. It takes a sadistic, "I told you so" glee in the potential suffering of others. There's an almost hopeful quality to it that's deeply unsettling. "Someday, you'll be sick and dying with a terrible illness, or you'll be in a terrifying accident, or the person you love most in the world will be gone from your life forever—and then I'll be proven right! Then you'll know the glory and majesty of the Lord! In your face!"

People will shamelessly and unhesitatingly say things about atheists that they would cringe from saying about people of different religions. Many believers—even progressive, ecumenical, "all religions have some truth and are all worshiping God in their own way" believers—will blithely say that atheists are immoral, that atheists have no meaning or joy in our lives, that atheists are just being trendy or rebellious, that atheists have no right to express our views in the public forum. And even the most zealous hard-core believers in their particular faith typically approach diverse religious beliefs with more tolerance than they show to atheism. Atheism seems to unsettle many believers, to a degree that different religious beliefs generally don't—and those believers seem perfectly willing to take out that unsettled feeling on atheists.

And the "no atheists in foxholes" trope is a classic example of this. It's not just a lie. It's not even just an ignorant, absurd, colossally dim-witted lie. It's a bigoted lie. It's a lie that denies our most basic humanity: the fact that atheists love life, that we're deeply attached to the people we love, and that we experience fear and grief in the face of death. It's a lie that tries to depict us, not just as callow and naive, but as something less than human.

If you're a believer: Please know that this is a lie.

And please don't tell it.

10

ATHEISM AND THE ARGUMENT
FROM COMFORT

"But religion offers people comfort. It makes people's lives easier. Why is it so important to you to convince people that it's wrong? Why are you trying to take that comfort away?"

I want to take on what I call "the argument from comfort." Or what my wife Ingrid, who at times is a bit more of a hard-ass than I am, tends to call "the argument from wishful thinking." It's an argument that tends to drive atheists batty—since it's not, in fact, an argument. It's an emotional defense for hanging onto an argument that's already been lost.

But more on that in a moment.

My first response to the argument from comfort would be: Religion doesn't universally offer comfort. In fact, it very often doesn't offer comfort. How much comfort does religion give to girls who've had their clitorises cut off because their religion requires it? To twelve year old rape victims being stoned to death for adultery? To abused wives being told by their religious leaders that it's their duty to stay in their abusive marriages? To people with AIDS in Africa who were denied access to condoms because the churches think condoms are sinful? To people being driven out of their villages, tortured, maimed, and even killed, because some preacher decided they were a witch? (And no, I don't mean in the 17th century—I mean today.)

You don't even have to go to those extremes. How much comfort does religion offer to very young children who are raised with vivid, terrifying images of being burned and tortured in Hell? To older children who are taught that their schoolmates will burn in Hell because they belong to the wrong religion? To teenagers who hate themselves because they're gay, and they've been taught that God despises them for it? To troubled married couples being counseled by priests and ministers and rabbis—who have no training in counseling or therapy, and who base their advice on religious dogma? To sick people being taught that God will heal them if they pray hard enough and have enough faith—and thus, by implication, being taught that if they don't get better, it's their fault? To old people near death, who live in terror that their children and grandchildren are going to burn in Hell because they left the faith? To anybody at all, of any age or situation, who's asking hard questions about their faith and who gets told by their religious leaders to simply stop asking?

But maybe I'm being too hard-assed. If someone is defending their religion by saying how much comfort they get from it, blasting its horrors is certainly fair—but it may not be the most effective rhetorical gambit in the world. It's likely to just put the believer on the defensive, and entrench them even further in their beliefs.

So that brings me to Argument #2: Atheism has its own comforts to offer.

Read some stories of deconversion. Many atheists do go through a dark night of the soul (or rather, a dark night of the soul-less) when they're giving up their religion. I certainly did. But they generally make it through that dark night. And once they do, they're generally happier, and feel like a burden has been lifted.

Atheism offers us the comfort of knowing that we can

shape our own lives, and don't have to rest our fate in the hands of a god whose ways can at best be described as "mysterious." It offers the comfort of not having to wonder what we did wrong, or why we're being punished or tested, every time something bad happens. It offers the comfort of experiencing the world as shaped by a stable and potentially comprehensible set of physical laws, rather than by the capricious whim of a creator who's theoretically loving but in practice is moody, short-tempered, and wildly unpredictable. It offers the comfort of being intimately connected with the rest of the universe, rather than somehow set apart from it. It offers the comfort of being able to make our own moral judgments, based on our own instincts and experiences, rather than trying to reconcile the outdated and self-contradictory teachings of a centuries-old religious text—or trying to second-guess the wishes of an invisible and imprecise deity. And it offers the comfort of being able to see the world as it is, to the best of our abilities, without having to ignore or rationalize every experience that contradicts our faith.

I will also point to the example of Europe. Many countries in Europe—France, England, the Netherlands, Scandinavian countries—have very high rates of atheism and agnosticism … and the people there aren't all walking around in the depths of despair. They're doing pretty well, actually (or as well as anybody is doing in the current lousy economy). They seem to have found a way to find comfort in the world, even in the face of death and other hardships, without needing to believe in God or an afterlife. It isn't just Europe, either: Japan also has high rates of religious non-belief, as do many cities and regions of the United States.

Now, as Ingrid points out: Death is something of a special case. The case for hard-nosed realism over comforting self-deception generally relies on the assumption that it's better to know the truth, because then you can act more effectively to solve the problem at hand. Death, however, is a problem that can't be solved. With care and effort and luck, death can often be postponed—but death is not a problem that can be fixed if we just have the courage to deal with its challenges head-on. Death is a problem that simply has to be faced, and accepted.

But even so, I would still argue for hard-nosed realism over comforting self-deception.

I would argue for it because the way you face the unsolvable problem of death makes a difference in how you live your life. If you live with the assumption that the single most important thing you can do with your life is to please God so you can go to Heaven when you die . . . you're going to live differently than if you think this life is the only life we have, and we therefore have to make the most of our opportunities and create as much joy as we can for ourselves and one another while we're here.

And if atheists are right, and there is no God and no afterlife, then all the time spent trying to appease a non-existent God and reach a non-existent blissful afterlife is purely wasted time. Unless it's time spent doing something that you'd find moral and valuable anyway, even if you didn't believe in God, then the comfort found in religion doesn't come free. It has a cost—the cost of wasted lives, bad decisions made based on a false premise.

And if a believer is making the argument from comfort, then they're essentially admitting that the premise they're basing their comfort on is false.

Which brings me to Number Three. Or rather, it brings me back around to where I started.

And that's this:

The argument from comfort is not an argument.

It is a sign of desperation.

It is a last-ditch effort to hang on to an argument that the believer knows in their heart—and may even know in their head—has already been lost.

I mean, if your big argument for religion is, "Sure,

it doesn't make sense, but wouldn't it be nice if it were true? Doesn't it make our lives easier to believe that it's true?"—you have effectively conceded the argument. That's not an argument for why religion is correct. It's not even trying to be an argument for why religion is correct. It's an argument for why it's okay to believe something that you know is almost certainly not true, but that you can't imagine living without.

So, from a rhetorical point of view: If someone is making the argument from comfort? In my opinion, that's the time to stop making arguments for why religion is highly implausible and atheism is probably true. They already know that. They've admitted as much.

That's the time, instead, to start softening the landing. That's the time to start pointing out the comforts that atheism does have to offer. That's the time to start pointing out positive atheist and humanist philosophies. That's the time to start pointing out all the atheists, throughout history and living today, who have led happy, productive, valuable lives. That's the time to start talking about the different ways that atheists cope with suffering and death, all the ways that we find meaning and joy and peace, without a belief in God or an afterlife. That's the time to start talking, not about why religion is incorrect, but about why it's unnecessary.

That's the time to stop making arguments, and to start offering comfort.

11

HUMANISM IN A SHITSTORM

I want to talk about a foxhole.

If you're a non-believer, I'm sure you've heard, more times than you care to remember, that there are no atheists in foxholes. I'm sure you've heard religious believers dismiss secular humanism as shallow, a breezily hedonistic philosophy that dries up and blows away in the face of trauma, mortality, and grief.

It's malarkey. You probably know that, of course: if you're an atheist, you probably know plenty of atheists who have been through terrible hardship without turning to religion. Chances are you've been through hardship yourself, with your godlessness intact. You may even know—or indeed be—an atheist in a literal foxhole;

not the metaphorical kind, but the actual military kind where they're trying to blow you up.

I want to talk about one of those metaphorical foxholes. I want to talk about how, in the depths of it, my atheism and humanism not only didn't dry up, but supported me and helped carry me through. And I want to encourage other humanists to talk, with each other and with religious believers, about your own trials and challenges—and the ways that humanism, atheism, materialism, skepticism, and an evidence-based view of the world have helped get you through. (Assuming, of course, that they have.)

The very short summary: In October of 2012, I got hit with a serious one-two punch. My father died early in the month—and less than two weeks later, I was diagnosed with uterine cancer.

Short of an actual military foxhole, this has got to be one of the most foxholey foxholes there is. If I saw this story in a movie, I wouldn't believe it. I'd think, "That is just insultingly manipulative. Who the hell gets diagnosed with cancer two weeks after their father dies? That doesn't happen to anyone." But it happened to me.

The cancer was treatable, and in fact has been treated. I got lucky there (if any kind of cancer can be "lucky"): the cancer was slow-growing, caught early, and entirely treated with hysterectomy, with no chemo or radiation needed. But it was still terrifying. Recovery from the surgery was slow, often painful, almost always difficult and exhausting. And it was much more traumatic coming so soon after my father's death. I was just barely beginning to recover from that shock, just barely beginning to wrestle with my grief, when the news about my cancer came. Plus there was a nasty feedback effect: each of these traumas left me weakened, and less able to cope with the other. (I was, for instance, keeping an almost-daily grief diary on my blog in the days after my father's death, which was helping me cope with that death and wring some meaning out of it—and which I had to abandon when the cancer came and immediately demanded all my attention.) And of course, the two traumas were closely entwined: the harsh realities of mortality and grief, of the eventual death of myself and everyone I love, were in my face every day, for weeks. Months, really.

If there were ever going to be a time when suffering, grief, and a stark reminder of my own mortality could make me turn to religion, this was it. And for days and weeks, I kept waiting for it. I didn't seriously think I would turn to religious belief—I know the arguments against it too thoroughly—but I kept waiting for the moment when I *wished* I believed. I kept waiting for the moment when I thought to myself, "Goddammit, this atheism stuff sucks. If only I believed in God or an afterlife, this would be so much easier." I kept waiting for that shoe to drop—and it kept not happening. The opposite has happened. The thought of religion has been making me queasy—and my humanism has been a profound comfort.

Honestly? If I believed in a god who made this shit happen on purpose, I wouldn't be comforted. I'd be wanting to find the biggest ladder I could, climb into Heaven, and punch the guy's lights out. Either that, or I'd be wracked with guilt and confusion trying to figure out what I'd done to deserve this, or what lesson I was supposed to be learning from it. If I had a relationship with an imaginary personal creator who supposedly loved me and yet made this horror show happen on purpose ... that would be just about the most toxic, fucked-up relationship I can imagine. I can't begin to see it as comforting. When I picture that relationship, what I feel is rage, guilt, confusion, and a poisonous mess of cognitive dissonance.

But it is tremendously comforting to see this horror show as physical cause and effect. My father didn't die, and I didn't get cancer, because some asshole in the sky was pulling the strings. My father died, and I got cancer, because of cause and effect in the natural world. And the unbelievably shitty timing of it? Physical cause and effect works that way sometimes. You roll a pair of dice long enough, chances are that at some point you're going to get snake-eyes. You live a long enough life, chances are that at some point you're going to get two or three horribly crappy things happening at once.

That can be hard to accept. It can be hard to accept that we often have little or no control over what happens to us. But when I compare the idea that "Yeah, sometimes life sucks, and I have to deal with it as best I can" with the idea that "An immensely powerful being is screwing with me on purpose and won't tell me why" . . . I, for one, find the first idea much more comforting. I don't have to torture myself with guilt over how I must have angered my god or screwed up my karma, with that guilt piling onto the trauma I'm already going through. And would the glib cliché that "everything happens for a reason" really give this shitstorm more meaning? Would it really be more comforting to twist my brain into absurd contortions trying to figure out what God was trying to teach me—and why the lesson was both so brutally enforced and so obscure?

Of course I can learn lessons from all this. I'm already

learning lessons from it. There's no way I'm going to be the same person after this shitstorm than I was before it. But *I* get to decide what lessons I learn from it. *I* get to infuse it with meaning. And that's the power I have. I don't have the pretend power that if I pray hard enough and do the right rituals to appease my imaginary friend, my life will always be awesome. What I do have is the real power to learn from the experiences that life hands me, and to use what I've learned to make myself a better person, and to make life better for others.

And the secular philosophies of death that I've been writing and reading and contemplating for years now . . . these have been a tremendous comfort. The idea I was astronomically lucky to have been born at all; the idea that my ideas will live on after I die; the idea that death is a deadline that helps focus my life and treasure it—in an unspeakably shitty time of my life, all these ideas and more have been a deep, solid, very real comfort. (The deadline one especially. When I first got the cancer diagnosis, one of my first reactions was, "I can't die! I have books to write!")

None of these humanist philosophies have made the trauma or grief magically disappear. Any more than prayer or belief in God magically makes trauma or grief magically disappear. When I say that these outlooks are comforting, I don't mean that they're a panacea. I mean that they staved off despair. They gave me a bridge over the chasm. When the worst of the fear and grief felt like it would overwhelm me, these outlooks gave me hope—a sense that life was worth returning to, and worth fighting for.

And that's not trivial.

When I first became a non-believer, I wasn't familiar with any of these ideas. I didn't even know that atheist or humanist communities existed. So I had to re-invent the wheel. I had to grind my own way to my godless views of life and death—and I had to go through my earliest experiences of godless hard times on my own. As a result, those hard times were much harder than they needed to be. I don't want anyone else to go through that. As hard as the weeks and months were after my cancer diagnosis and my father's death, they were made far, far easier by the ideas I've learned, and the skills I've acquired, and the connections and friendships I've formed, from my years in the humanist and atheist and skeptical communities.

So let's talk about this. Let's not concede the ground of comfort to the religious. Let's talk about the worst of times—and how humanism can help get us through. Let's give other people who are questioning their faith, and other people who have let go of their faith and are going through hard times, a hand across the chasm, and a safe place to land.

RESOURCE GUIDE

This is not a thorough guide to resources available to atheists. You can find one of those on my blog, reprinted from my previous book *Coming Out Atheist: How to Do It, How to Help Each Other, and Why*, at: freethoughtblogs. com/greta/2014/02/12/coming-out-atheist-resource-guide/. Unlike that guide, this is a short list of a few of the resources available to atheists who are grieving or who are struggling with mortality and death.

Grief Beyond Belief
Faith-free support for non-religious people grieving the death of a loved one.
Website: griefbeyondbelief.org
Facebook group: facebook.com/faithfreegriefsupport
Grief Beyond Belief Forums: griefbeyondbelief.org/forums-description

Grief Beyond Belief List of Secular and Humanist Funeral Officiants: griefbeyondbelief.org/resources/#secular&humanistfuneralofficiants

Grief Beyond Belief List of Secular Funerals and Memorials—Information and Sample Ceremonies: griefbeyondbelief.org/resources/#secularfunerals&memorials

Grief Beyond Belief Secular Grief Library: griefbeyondbelief.org/library

Choice In Dying
Arguing for the right to die and against the religious obstruction of that right.
choiceindying.com

Coping With Illness & Disability, Without Faith
A Facebook page for people who have chronic illnesses and disabilities and have learned that we don't need faith to get through it, because we know that the strength that gets us through comes from us. If you're tired of being told "It's God's plan!" then this page is for you!
https://www.facebook.com/groups/327120207356544/

A Grief Workbook for Skeptics, **by Carol Fiore**
Written by an atheist who watched her husband die,

this workbook combines a guided journal with self-help tools. Author Carol Fiore leads the reader through chapters designed specifically for the nonbeliever, such as how to handle statements like "God has a plan." She addresses the power of nature, the healing role of pets, setting up memorials, doing volunteer work, re-creating yourself without your loved one, and more.

Mortality, by Christopher Hitchens

Throughout the course of his ordeal battling esophageal cancer, Hitchens adamantly and bravely refused the solace of religion, preferring to confront death with both eyes open. In this riveting account of his affliction, Hitchens poignantly describes the torments of illness, discusses its taboos, and explores how disease transforms experience and changes our relationship to the world around us.

Secular Therapist Project

A confidential service matching nonbelievers looking for therapy with secular therapists: therapists who are nonbelievers or are committed to providing secular, evidence-based therapy that does not involve super-natural or religious elements. The service is confidential for both patients and therapists.

seculartherapy.org

ABOUT THE AUTHOR

Greta Christina is the author of *Coming Out Atheist: How to Do It, How to Help Each Other, and Why*; *Why Are You Atheists So Angry? 99 Things That Piss Off the Godless*; and *Bending: Dirty Kinky Stories About Pain, Power, Religion, Unicorns, & More*, and is editor of *Paying for It: A Guide by Sex Workers for Their Clients*. She has been a public speaker for many years, and is on the speaker's bureaus of the Secular Student Alliance and Center for Inquiry. She is a regular contributor to *AlterNet*, *Free Inquiry*, the *Humanist*, and *Salon*. Her writing has appeared in magazines and newspapers including the *Chicago Sun-Times*, *Ms.*, *On Our Backs*, *Penthouse*, and *Skeptical Inquirer*, and anthologies including *Everything You Know About God Is Wrong* and three volumes of *Best American Erotica*. She lives in San Francisco.